NATIONAL
GEOGRAPHIC

Travels Across America's Pa.

The Southwest
Its History and People

Adam McClellam

Picture Credits
Cover (top), pages 6 (bottom right), 7 (top left) Hulton-Archive/Getty Images; cover (bottom) Kelly Mooney Photography/Corbis; pages 1, 6 (bottom left), 8, 12-13 Smithsonian American Art Museum/Art Resource, NY; pages 2-3 Buffalo Bill Historical Center, Cody, WY, 7.69; pages 4 (top), 30 (top) Joseph Sohm, ChromoSohm Inc./Corbis; pages 4 (bottom), 6 (top), 6 (bottom middle), 7 (bottom middle), 11 (top), 14, 17, 19 (bottom), 20 (bottom left) Corbis; pages 4-5 Imagebank/Getty Images; pages 6-7 Bridgeman Art Library/Getty Images; pages 7 (top right), 16, 20-21, 21 (middle), 22-23, 25 (bottom), 28 Bettmann/Corbis; page 7 (bottom left) courtesy Library of Congress; pages 7 (bottom right), 9, 31 (background) David Meunch/Corbis; page 10 (background) Greg Probst/Corbis; page 10 (inset) Bob Rowan, Progressive Image/Corbis; page 11 (bottom) Philbrook Museum of Art, Tulsa, OK; pages 15 (bottom), 27 (right) taxi/Getty Images; page 15 (top) Print and Photograph Collection, CN01405, Center for American History, University of Texas; pages 18-19 George H. H. Huey/Corbis; page 21 (top) Gilcrease Museum, Tulsa, OK; page 24 Richard Cummins/Corbis; pages 25 (top), 32 Charles & Josette Lenars/Corbis; pages 26-27 Roger Cooke Fine Arts/ALVA Mural Society; page 29 Courtesy/Texas Energy Museum, Beaumont, TX; page 30 (bottom) Tim Thompson/Corbis; page 30 (inset) courtesy Powell Museum.

Maps: pages 5, 18, 20 Sue Carlson

Produced through the worldwide resources of the National Geographic Society, John M. Fahey, Jr., President and Chief Executive Officer; Gilbert M. Grosvenor, Chairman of the Board; Nina D. Hoffman, Executive Vice President and President, Books and School Publishing.

Prepared by National Geographic School Publishing
Ericka Markman, Senior Vice President; Steve Mico, Vice President, Editorial Director; Marianne Hiland, Editorial Manager; Jim Hiscott, Design Manager; Kristin Hanneman, Illustrations Manager; Matt Wascavage, Manager of Publishing Services; Sean Philpotts, Production Manager.

Production: Clifton M. Brown III, Manufacturing and Quality Control

Program Development
Gare Thompson Associates, Inc.

Book Development
Thomas Nieman, Inc.

Consultants/Reviewers
Dr. Margit E. McGuire, School of Education, Seattle University, Seattle, Washington

Book Design
Steven Curtis Design, Inc.

Copyright © 2003 National Geographic Society. All Rights Reserved. Reproduction in whole or in part of the contents without written permission from the publisher is prohibited.

National Geographic Society, National Geographic School Publishing, National Geographic Reading Expeditions, and the Yellow Border are registered trademarks of the National Geographic Society.

Published by the National Geographic Society
1145 17th Street, N.W.
Washington, D.C. 20036-4688

ISBN 0-7922-8619-7

Second Printing March 2018
Printed in the United States of America

Table of Contents

Introduction

Meet Your Guide to the Southwest

$\mathcal{H}$i, my name is Inez. I'm from the sunny Southwest. I'll be your guide as we visit this wonderful region and learn about its history and its people.

The Southwest today is home to many different peoples. Native Americans were here first. Then Spanish explorers came, followed by settlers from Mexico. Much later, Americans came to the Southwest.

There's a lot of wealth underground here. There's oil in Texas and Oklahoma. In Arizona and New Mexico, there's copper, silver, and uranium.

Today, the Southwest is one of the fastest growing regions in the country. Many people move here for jobs. Others choose to retire here in the sun.

So that's the Southwest as it is today. But what was it like long ago? Come along and find out.

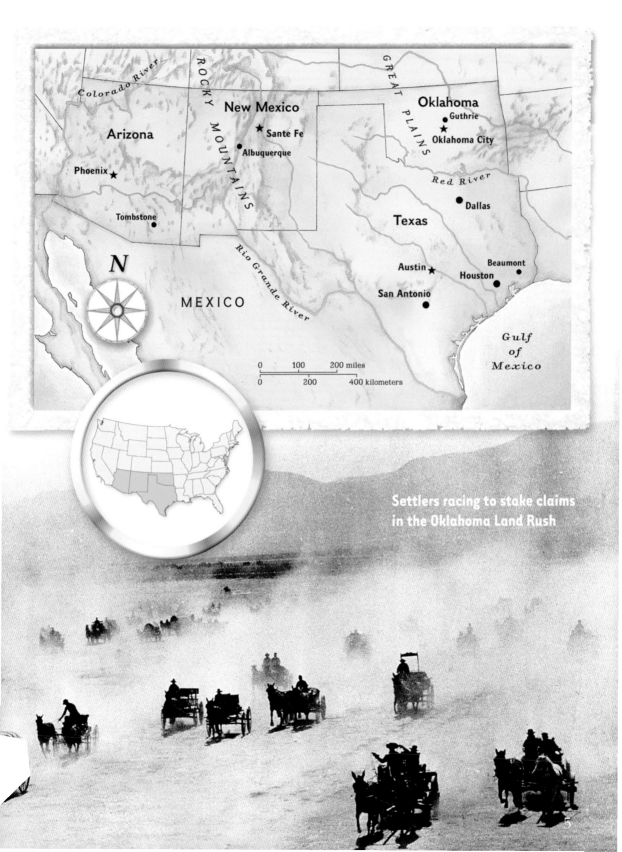

Arizona

Phoenix ★

Tombstone ●

Colorado River

ROCKY MOUNTAINS

New Mexico

★ Sante Fe

● Albuquerque

GREAT PLAINS

Oklahoma

● Guthrie

★ Oklahoma City

Red River

● Dallas

Texas

Rio Grande River

MEXICO

Austin ★

San Antonio ●

Houston ●

Beaumont ●

Gulf of Mexico

N

0   100   200 miles

0   200   400 kilometers

Settlers racing to stake claims
in the Oklahoma Land Rush

Time Line
of the Southwest

The Southwest has a long history. Here are some key events from its past. I'll tell you more about many of them as we go along.

1610
Santa Fe founded.

··· *1500* ··········· *1600* ········ *1700* ···· *1725* ···· *1750* ···· *1775*

▲
1492
Columbus's first voyage

▲
1775–1783
American Revolution

1540–1542
Coronado
expedition

By 1500
Hopi culture
has become
highly developed.

1821
Stephen Austin
arrives in Texas.

6

1821
Santa Fe
Trail opens.

1836
Texas wins
independence.

| 1800 | 1825 | 1850 | 1875 | 1900 | 1925 | 1950 |

▲ | ▲ | | ▲ | ▲

1846–1848 | **1861–1865** | **1914–1918** | **1939–1945**
Mexican-American War | **Civil War** | **World War I** | **World War II**

1867
Big cattle
drives begin.

1901
Oil discovered
at Spindletop.

1889
First Oklahoma
Land Rush

A Hopi woman

Three Cultures

*N*ative American peoples have lived in the Southwest for thousands of years. They were here long before Columbus came to America. Some, such as the **Anasazi**, built villages and farmed the lands around them. But the Anasazi left their homes around the year 1300. No one knows why they disappeared. Other peoples, such as the Zuni, Pueblo, and **Hopi**, stayed and farmed in the Southwest.

In the 1500s, Spain established **colonies** in the New World. Spanish explorers went into the Southwest in search of gold and other riches. In 1610, Spanish settlers founded the city of Santa Fe. Other towns followed. Soon there were many Spanish settlements.

In the early 1800s, settlers from the United States were moving westward. Beginning in 1821, Americans started settling in Texas. Texas at that time belonged to Mexico. Soon the Americans in Texas outnumbered the Mexican settlers.

Let's visit the Southwest during these early times. First, let's go to a **pueblo,** or village. The Hopi live there. Let's see what life was like for them in the 1700s.

A Hopi pot

9

A Hopi Pueblo, 1700s

We're in a Hopi pueblo in what is now Arizona. The village is high on a **mesa**, or flat-topped mountain. Living on a mountain is safe, because the Hopi can see enemies a long way off. Low buildings of **adobe**, or sunbaked mud bricks, make up the village. The most important part of the pueblo is the **kiva**. It is an underground room where special religious rites for men are held.

Ruins of an ancient
Hopi pueblo

The Hopi farm in the valleys below the mesa. They build low walls to protect their crops from animals. Their fields are planted with beans and squash. But the most important crop is corn. The Hopi eat corn in many different ways. Sometimes, they roast whole ears in an open fire. Other times, they grind the dried kernels into meal. They use the meal to make mush or bread.

When they plant corn, the Hopi use a stick to dig a deep hole. Sometimes it is as much as a foot and a half into the earth.

This is so the corn's roots will be able to reach underground water. Then they throw in a handful of seeds. They might put as many as 20 seeds into each hole. That way, there's a good chance that at least one of them will grow.

The corn harvest is the time for many celebrations. There are dances, ceremonies, and lots of food. For now, the Hopi remain apart from the Spanish, who are settling the Southwest. But towns are growing up in this region. Let's visit a Spanish town and see what life is like there.

Nampeyo

People of the Southwest

Nampeyo was a Hopi woman born in what is now Arizona around 1860. She loved ancient Anasazi pottery. She searched for different clays and unusual ways to mix and bake the clay. She gave new life to the ancient designs and created a new kind of pottery for the Hopi.

Hopi corn dance

Albuquerque, 1782

In 1782, the little Spanish colonial town of Albuquerque is a cluster of adobe houses along the Rio Grande. Let's go inside the Vega family's home. It's hot outside, but thick walls keep things cool inside. The floor is just packed earth covered by a simple wool rug woven by Señora Vega.

Señor Vega works as a **blacksmith**. He makes iron horseshoes for the many horses here. He also makes tools. His wife takes care of the house and looks after the children. She is cooking a stew of meat and beans. The family will eat their meal with corn **tortillas**. Like the Hopi, most New Mexican farmers grow corn. They also grow peppers and beans and raise sheep. The sheep provide meat and wool for clothes and rugs.

Slowly, more people move into the Southwest. The United States becomes interested in this land too. Stephen Austin wants to settle American families in the Spanish province of Texas. Let's see how his plan works out.

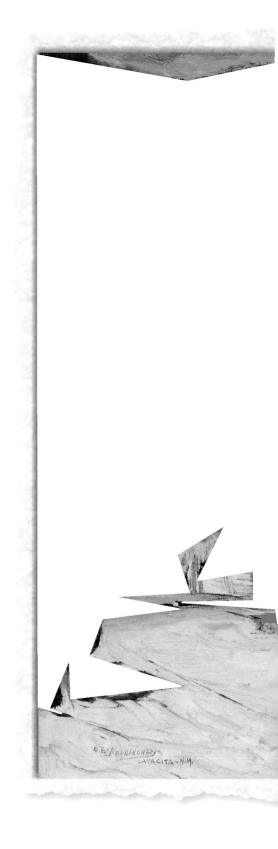

A harvest of red peppers brightens a New Mexican town.

12

Texas, 1820s

It's 1822 and we're in Texas, standing beside a river. Nearby, a small, dark-haired man talks with a group of people. His name is Stephen Austin. He has brought American families to settle in the rich farmlands here. Mexico has given him 200 thousand acres to settle. In return, Austin has promised that the 300 families he brings will be loyal to Mexico.

Now it's September of 1825. Time has passed since the first families settled. Over 270 families have already settled here. Stephen Austin has built a town. Those two log cabins are Austin's houses. He lives in one. He governs the small colony from another.

Map of Texas drawn by Stephen Austin in 1822

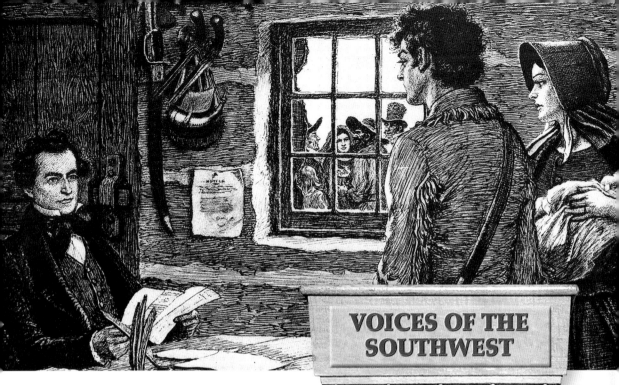

Stephen Austin with Texas settlers

Look, another family is arriving! First, the father hands Austin a letter. It states that this new settler has good morals and is hardworking. Austin reads the letter. He then leads the family in an oath of loyalty to Mexico. Finally, he issues a permit. The permit gives them 30 days to look around the colony and choose their land. Each day more families arrive. Soon, the Americans outnumber the Mexicans.

So now you have seen all the different peoples that settled in the Southwest. But not all the land was settled. Let's see what life was like in the wide open country.

VOICES OF THE SOUTHWEST

Stephen Austin

Austin fell in love with Texas. He thought it was the most beautiful place on earth.

"The country back of this place and below for about 15 miles (as far as we went) is as good in every respect as man could wish for, land all first rate—plenty of timber, fine water—beautifully rolling."

15

The United States and Mexico continued to settle parts of the Southwest. Towns, farms, and ranches sprang up in Texas and parts of New Mexico.

But as more people settled in the Southwest, conflicts broke out. In 1835, Americans in Texas rebelled, and Texas became independent. In 1845, it joined the United States. Then, the United States went to war with Mexico. Mexico lost the war, and New Mexico and Arizona also became part of the United States. But whoever owned it, much of the Southwest was still wide open country.

Traders passed through the Southwest along the Santa Fe Trail. Mexico first let American traders come to Santa Fe in 1821. Over time, millions of dollars worth of goods moved across the dusty country from Missouri to New Mexico. Traders from both countries made a good living.

Traders weren't the only ones moving through the Southwest. Cowboys drove huge herds of cattle out of Texas to railroads in Missouri and Kansas. These cattle drives gave us one of the best known symbols of America— the cowboy.

Let's saddle up and hit the Santa Fe Trail.

Arizona cowboys in the late 1870s

The Santa Fe Trail, 1833

It's late spring in 1833, and we're jolting along in a wagon down the Santa Fe Trail. The **wagon train** left Missouri 50 days ago. The trail stretches 780 miles across the prairie. Traders use it to travel between the United States and Mexico. The wagons around us are full of goods that people are hoping to sell in Santa Fe. There's everything from tables and chairs to spices and tobacco. Some of the traders will even sell their wagons before they're done!

Finally, we reach Santa Fe. The people who live here have come out to see us, calling *"Los Americanos!"* They're excited to see the goods the traders have brought. The traders set up shop for the summer in the great central plaza, or public square, of Santa Fe. Some will sell their goods for gold and silver Mexican coins. Others will trade for goods that they think will sell well back in the United States.

Remains of the Santa Fe Trail

The Santa Fe Trail

Missouri

Unorganized Territory

GREAT PLAINS

Independence

ROCKY MOUNTAINS

N

MEXICO

Santa Fe

0   100   200 miles
0   200   400 kilometers

Arkansas Territory

18

Look at the people leaving. They are Mexican traders on their way to Missouri. The Santa Fe Trail is a crowded, busy place as the traders make their way to and from Santa Fe. The traffic on the trail goes on until 1880 when the railroad is built. Let's try another trail. Get out your cowboy hat, for we're going on a cattle drive up the Chisholm Trail.

Traders crossing the mountains on the Santa Fe Trail

Susan Shelby Magoffin

People of the Southwest

In June of 1846, a young woman named Susan Shelby Magoffin began riding down the Santa Fe Trail with her husband Samuel, a trader. She was one of the first women from the United States to travel the trail. Her diary gives a lively account of what she saw.

The Chisholm Trail, 1872

Stay on your horse. We're riding alongside hundreds of head of **Texas longhorns**. Cowboys are driving the cattle north along the Chisholm Trail to the railroad at Abilene, Kansas. The front of a moving herd is called the "point." The rear is called the "drag." Up front, two point men keep the herd moving in the right direction. Far behind us in the drag, other cowboys round up any stragglers.

Each year, cowboys drive hundreds of thousands of longhorns over cattle trails out of Texas on their way to market. The cowboys' work is always hard and often risky. Their days are long, and at night they must take turns watching the cattle. Longhorns are half-wild, bad-tempered animals with huge, sharply pointed horns. Weather on the range varies from great heat to blinding blizzards. During a storm, thunder and lightning can start a deadly stampede. **Rustlers** and Indians are a danger.

The Chisholm Trail

0   300 miles
0   400 kilometers

Denver
Colorado Territory
Kansas
Ellsworth   Abilene
Missouri
Arkansas
New Mexico Territory
Indian Territory
Texas
San Antonio
Louisiana
N

Cowboys sitting around a chuck wagon

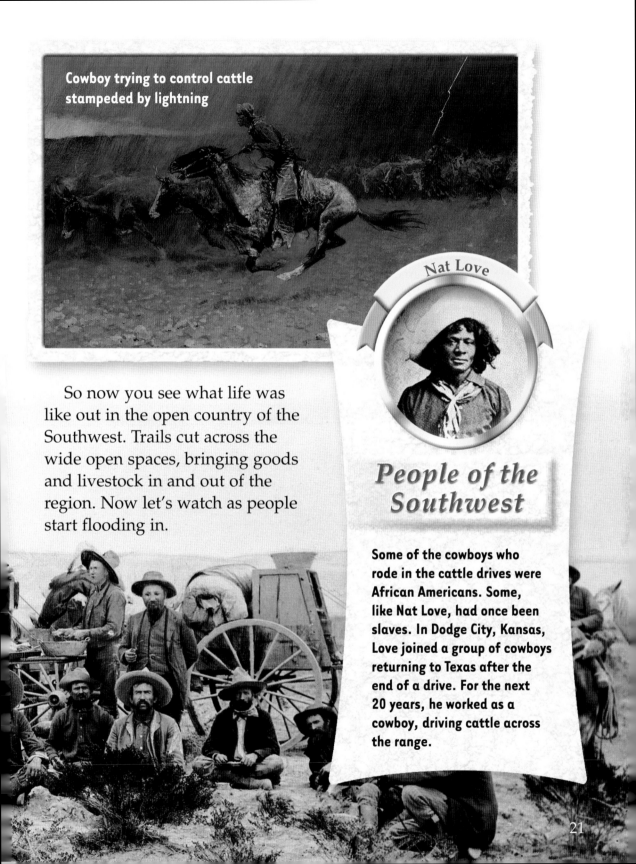

Cowboy trying to control cattle stampeded by lightning

Nat Love

So now you see what life was like out in the open country of the Southwest. Trails cut across the wide open spaces, bringing goods and livestock in and out of the region. Now let's watch as people start flooding in.

People of the Southwest

Some of the cowboys who rode in the cattle drives were African Americans. Some, like Nat Love, had once been slaves. In Dodge City, Kansas, Love joined a group of cowboys returning to Texas after the end of a drive. For the next 20 years, he worked as a cowboy, driving cattle across the range.

$\mathcal{M}$ore people came to the Southwest in the late 1800s. Some came to strike it rich. Others came looking for land or work. But all of them saw opportunities in the region.

Spindletop oil field near Beaumont, Texas

There had been earlier settlers here. They were Native American peoples forced from their homelands east of the Mississippi River. The U.S. government had promised that these lands would always be theirs. But when Americans saw the lands, they wanted them. And the government went back on its word.

Silver strikes drew miners to the Southwest. Boomtowns grew up almost overnight. One was Tombstone, Arizona, where silver was discovered in 1877.

Thousands of people flocked to Tombstone. It was a sometimes rough, but often exciting, place to live.

In 1889, thousands more people came to Oklahoma seeking land. At noon, on April 22, the Oklahoma District was opened to settlement. Land was up for grabs. The first person to claim a piece of land kept it.

Fifty thousand people raced in there that day. They wanted land and a better life. Additional land rushes brought more people to Oklahoma to settle.

But nothing topped the oil boom that began near Beaumont, Texas, on January 10, 1901. The discovery of oil brought people running, first to Beaumont, then to other parts of Texas and Oklahoma. All hoped to strike it rich. The discovery of oil changed the economy of the Southwest forever.

So let's head off to Tombstone, for a look at a boomtown! You may want to keep a sharp watch—there are some rough characters around.

Tombstone, 1881

The year is 1881, and we're in one of the biggest silver mining towns in the Southwest. A short time ago, a **prospector** came here looking for silver. The soldiers stationed nearby said all he would find would be his own tombstone. Instead, he struck it rich! He decided that *Tombstone* would make a fine name for the site.

You might expect that a mining town would be full of rough men living in tents. At first, that's what Tombstone was like. But now, the town has *two* newspapers! There are fine hotels and restaurants, ice-cream parlors, theaters, a photo studio, and tennis courts. There's even a bowling alley. Of course, there are also plenty of saloons and gambling halls. The miners go there to spend their wealth. And there is also crime—cattle rustling, stagecoach robberies, and gunfights.

Miners brought samples of ore to the Tombstone assay office to find out how much silver they contained.

The most famous gunfight in the history of the Old West took place behind Tombstone's OK Corral on the afternoon of October 26, 1881.

On one side was a local lawman, Virgil Earp. With him were his brothers Wyatt and Morgan and their friend John "Doc" Holliday. On the other side were five local tough guys. They were Tom and Frank McLaury, Ike and Billy Clanton, and Billy Claiborne. The fight lasted 30 seconds. When it was over, the McLaurys and Billy Clanton were dead. Virgil and Morgan Earp and Doc Holliday were wounded.

People of the Southwest

Wyatt Earp was one of the most famous lawmen of the Old West. Before he came to Tombstone, he had been on the police force of the tough cow towns of Wichita and Dodge City, Kansas. He left Tombstone in 1882. He later went to Los Angeles, where he worked as a consultant on several Western movies.

25

Settlers racing to stake claims in the Oklahoma Land Rush

Oklahoma Land Rush, 1889

It's April 22, 1889. Hundreds of people on horses, in wagons, and on foot are waiting for a gunshot to signal the opening of the Oklahoma District. In the next 24 hours, two million acres of land, once promised to the Native Americans, can be claimed by settlers.

The U.S. Army has tried to clear the district of all citizens to make the rush for land fairer. But some people, called "sooners," have hidden in the woods and along the creeks.

These sooners will get many of the best sites. Bang! The land rush is on! Hundreds speed across the low, rolling hills. The first person to reach a homestead or town lot claims it.

Now, we're walking the streets of Guthrie, Oklahoma. Hundreds of tents have sprung up on what was once open country. Some belong to people who raced in from the border this morning. By the time the sun sets, Guthrie is a bustling place with more than 10,000 people.

In the coming years, more and more Native American land is opened in other land rushes. Included among the new settlers are African Americans, giving Oklahoma a large black population from its early days onward. In 1907, Oklahoma becomes the 46th state.

Land wasn't the only thing that could bring people running. Let's go to Spindletop Hill in Texas and watch how a gush of oil changes a region.

VOICES OF THE SOUTHWEST

William Willard Howard

An observer at the Oklahoma Land Rush told how one settler got his claim.

"One man left the line with the others, carrying on his back a tent, a blanket, some camp dishes, an axe, and food for 2 days. He ran down the railway for 6 miles, and reached his claim in just 60 minutes. Upon arriving on his land he fell down under a tree, unable to speak or see. I am glad to be able to say that his claim is one of the best in Oklahoma."

Beaumont, early 1900s

It's January 10, 1901, and we're standing on Spindletop, a hill near Beaumont, Texas. Three men stand around an oil **derrick**. That's the tall framework that supports the drilling rig busily boring into the ground. Suddenly, the earth rumbles. The men scatter. A huge stream of mud shoots out of the hole. It sends the drill pipe flying into the air. The men watch and wait as the stream slows and then dies. Carefully, they walk back to the hole. Then there's a sound like a cannon shot and another stream of mud. Natural gas trapped in the well explodes, knocking the men down. At last, a six-inch-thick stream of dark, heavy liquid pours out—oil!

The Spindletop gusher is by far the biggest ever seen in Texas—or the United States, for that matter. Soon, people from all over are flocking to Beaumont, seeking their fortune. Let's jump ahead to 1902 and see what's happened.

The gusher at Spindletop

Tens of thousands of people have poured into Beaumont. The city has had some trouble keeping up with the rapid growth. Don't drink the water! It will give you painful stomach cramps. The folks around here call them "the Beaumonts." Still, people keep coming. More derricks have sprung up on Spindletop. People have started exploring and drilling all over the area. Land prices have skyrocketed.

A clerk who bought four acres of land for $60 a couple of years ago was able to resell them for $100,000! Beaumont is a town swimming in money and oil.

Other oil boomtowns will follow. Oil will become one of the most important industries in the Southwest. But Beaumont is the last stop on our tour. It's time to say goodbye to the Southwest's past.

Oil derricks at Spindletop in 1903

Yesterday and Today

We've seen some important events in the history of the Southwest and met some of its people. By now, I hope you have a sense of why I'm so proud to call the Southwest home!

Many traditions live on in the Southwest. Native Americans here still make fine pottery. And Southwest cooking, with its Mexican flavors, is wonderful. There are no more cattle drives, but people visit our big ranches.

Others attend **rodeos**. And many people visit the Santa Fe Trail to see where the traders traveled long ago.

Today, the Southwest continues to grow. Oil is still big, but many other businesses are too. Austin, Texas, and Phoenix, Arizona, are among the leading high-tech centers in the nation.

You'll understand the Southwest today better if you know its past. I hope you liked our trip. Adios!

Cowgirl riding in a
Southwestern rodeo

Then & Now
Glen Canyon Dam

In 1869, John Wesley Powell led a group of men on a risky journey to explore the wild Colorado River. Completed in 1966, Arizona's Glen Canyon Dam has helped to tame the river.

Glossary

adobe sunbaked mud brick

Anasazi a Native American people living in the Southwest from about A.D. 100 to 1300

blacksmith a person who shapes iron into horseshoes, tools, and other objects

colony a territory ruled by a foreign government

derrick a tall framework that supports an oil drilling rig

Hopi a Native American people of the Southwest

kiva an underground room in a Hopi pueblo where special religious rites for men are held

mesa a flat-topped mountain

prospector a person who explores an area for valuable minerals, such as gold, silver, and oil

pueblo a Native American village in the Southwest

rodeo a show in which cowboy skills of riding and roping are displayed

rustler a cattle thief

Texas longhorn Southwestern breed of cattle with long, curved horns

tortilla a round, flat Mexican bread made from cornmeal or wheat flour

wagon train a line of wagons traveling cross-country

Anasazi cliff dwelling at Mesa Verde